Money First, Love Second

A Blueprint for Financial Independence

James Royce Smartman

Copyright © 2024 James Royce Smartman

All rights reserved.

DEDICATION

To individuals who have the courage to pursue their dreams and the freedom that comes with becoming financially independent. I hope you have the fortitude to put your objectives first, the discernment to handle life's challenges, and the bravery to confidently embrace love. To all the trailblazers paving their own routes to success, this book is dedicated. I hope your journey is rewarding and your future is bright.

CONTENTS

ACKNOWLEDGMENTS..1

CHAPTER 1...1

The Power of Financial Independence... 1

    1.1 The Importance of Money Over Love.. 1

    1.2 How Financial Security Affects Life Decisions................................ 3

    1.3 The Advantages of Financial Independence for the Mind................5

CHAPTER 2...9

Establishing a Firm Financial Basis.. 9

    2.1 Successful Budgeting..9

    2.2 The Secret to Long-Term Stability: Savings...................................12

    2.3 Putting Money Into Your Future...15

CHAPTER 3...19

Financial Development and Career Advancement.......................19

    3.1 Selecting a Professional Route for Monetary Achievement........... 19

    3.2 Ascending the Corporate Ladder...22

    3.3 Entrepreneurism and Side Projects...25

CHAPTER 4...29

Managing Financial Risks.. 29

    4.1 The Significance of Insurance in Budgeting...................................29

    4.2 Avoiding Financial Pitfalls... 33

    4.3 Emergency Financial Planning... 36

CHAPTER 5...40

Developing Lifelong Financial Management Skills......................40

    5.1 Tools and Software for Personal Finance.................................. 40

    5.2 Building Sound Financial Practices... 44

    5.3 The Function of Financial Consultants.................................... 47

CHAPTER 6..52

Management and Removal of Debt...52

    6.1 Comprehending Various Debt Types..................................... 52

    6.2 Debt Repayment Techniques.. 56

    6.3 Preventing Recurrence of Debt... 59

CHAPTER 7..64

Long-Term Financial Planning..64

    7.1 Retirement Planning..64

    7.2 Estee Planning and Will Creation... 68

    7.3 Optimization and Tax Planning.. 72

CHAPTER 8..77

Juggling Finances and Relationships...77

    8.1 The Discussion of Money in Partnerships............................. 77

    8.2 Keeping a Relationship Financially Independent................. 80

    8.3 Resolving Conflicts, Love, and Money.................................. 83

CHAPTER 9..87

The Economic Effects of Important Life Choices............................ 87

    9.1 Purchasing vs. Renting a Home.. 87

    9.2 Financial Aspects of Beginning a Family...............................92

    9.3 Financial Planning and Major Life Transitions.................... 94

CHAPTER 10..99

The Path to Financial Independence... 99

10.1 How to Define Financial Independence..99

10.2 Prior to falling in love, Achieving Financial Independence....... 102

10.3 Maintaining Economic Achievement... 104

ABOUT THE AUTHOR..108

ACKNOWLEDGMENTS

Please accept my sincere gratitude to all those who have contributed to the writing of this book. I want to express my gratitude to my family and friends for their unfailing support and encouragement; your faith in me has always inspired me.

I would especially like to thank the mentors and financial professionals who have helped me form my idea of financial freedom by sharing their knowledge and insights. The content in these pages has been crafted with the help of your wisdom.

I also want to thank my readers, whose insatiable curiosity and dedication to self-improvement motivate me to keep learning and sharing. I hope this book helps you on your path to financial independence.

Finally, I would like to express my gratitude to the hardworking editors, designers, and everyone else who helped make my idea a reality. This book is a result of your diligence and imagination.

We appreciate your support and donations, everyone. By working together, we can enable others and ourselves to become financially independent and lead satisfying lives.

CHAPTER 1

THE POWER OF FINANCIAL INDEPENDENCE

Being financially independent is essential to leading a successful and satisfying life. Prior to committing to long-term relationships or other obligations, it is crucial to attain financial security. It improves your capacity to make choices that support your individual objectives and lays a more solid, wholesome basis for partnerships in the future. This chapter will examine the importance of putting financial independence first, how it affects choices in life, and the psychological advantages of reaching financial independence.

1.1 The Importance of Money Over Love

A key component of human growth is financial stability. Although relationships and love are important parts of life, they frequently thrive when they have a solid financial base. This is the reason:

Examining how crucial financial security is to one's personal growth:

Being financially secure frees you up to concentrate on developing your dreams, growing as a person, and learning about yourself. You can invest in hobbies, education, and professional advancement without being distracted by financial concern, which eventually boosts your self-esteem and sense of fulfillment in life. Being able to support yourself increases your sense of independence, which makes you less susceptible to other pressures.

Comprehending the liberty and prospects that accompany financial autonomy:

Being financially independent gives you the freedom to choose your living situation, leisure activities, and professional options. With this independence, you can live your life as you see fit, free from the limitations of financial reliance. Financial independence makes it possible to pursue opportunities that might not have been possible otherwise, such as traveling, launching a business, or going back to school.

Securing your financial future will help you build a solid foundation for future relationships.

Balance is brought about by entering a partnership with financial stability. It guarantees that your partnership is based on respect for one another rather than reliance and lessens the possibility that financial hardship will become a cause of contention. Making sure you have a stable financial future before you fall in love guarantees that you are contributing to the relationship as an equal partner rather than as someone in need of financial assistance.

Prioritizing financial independence creates the foundation for a more balanced, healthy, and courteous relationship free from the power dynamics that frequently result from financial imbalance.

1.2 How Financial Security Affects Life Decisions

Being financially independent has an impact on your present as well as how your future develops. Here are some ways that having money might change the way you make choices:

How being financially independent enables you to make better choices in life:

When you are financially secure, you are not influenced by short-term financial demands and can instead base decisions on your long-term objectives and personal values. You can establish a business or follow your passion, for instance, and take measured career risks without worrying about becoming bankrupt. You may make decisions in life with clarity and purpose when you have this autonomy, and your decisions will be in line with your own goals and vision.

Being financially independent to prevent reliance on others:

Being financially independent lessens the need to depend on others for financial support, including friends, family, and partners. This independence encourages you to make your own decisions. Because your financial stability is independent of other people or organizations, it allows you the freedom to quit unhealthy conditions, such as unsatisfactory work or personal relationships. Knowing that you are in charge of your own destiny also promotes a sense of empowerment.

The relationship in contemporary culture between personal freedom and wealth:

Nowadays, having money is frequently equated with having freedom. You can live your life as you see fit when you are financially independent. Having money allows you the freedom to design a life that aligns with your goals and values, whether that means deciding where to live, how to spend your time, or which causes to support. You may invest in life-enhancing activities, take time off for personal growth, and follow your passions when you are not burdened by money.

Because independent decisions are motivated by sincere intent rather than necessity, having this ability improves not only your quality of life but also your capacity to establish and preserve important, happy relationships.

1.3 The Advantages of Financial Independence for the Mind

Gaining financial independence has significant

psychological advantages that enhance your general sense of wellbeing, lower stress levels, and improve mental health:

Examining the mental clarity that comes with having money:

For many people, having financial security removes a significant cause of concern. The ongoing concern about providing for necessities like food, housing, and medical care goes away when one is financially independent. This alleviation clears your mind so you may concentrate on your career and personal development. When financial worries no longer influence your decisions, mental clarity arises, allowing you to face life with focus and clarity.

How lowering financial stress improves general health:

One of the main reasons for worry and conflict in relationships is financial stress. The stress of living paycheck to paycheck, accruing debt, or depending on others for support is eliminated when you achieve financial independence. As a result of this stress reduction, both mental and physical health improve. According to studies, those who are financially stable have reduced anxiety and depression levels, which immediately enhances their quality of life. You can develop better sleep habits, happier relationships, and a more optimistic view of life when you have less worries.

Enhancing self-assurance with economic empowerment:
Being financially independent makes you feel more confident. You feel more equipped to handle life's obstacles when you are in charge of your finances. Knowing that you can manage unforeseen losses, make wise financial decisions, and take care of yourself gives you a sense of empowerment. Being economically empowered also makes you feel more valuable because you realize how much you can give to society and your own life. This self-assurance is frequently seen in other spheres of life, such as your relationships and profession.

Achieving financial independence is a life-changing process that affects all facets of your existence, not just a goal. You can make sure that you enter partnerships as a self-assured, independent person who can contribute equally and meaningfully by putting your financial security before your romantic interests. In addition to providing the psychological advantages of less stress, more clarity, and more self-confidence, financial independence enables you to make deliberate, well-informed decisions in your life. Achieving financial independence is essential to gaining personal contentment and fostering successful relationships in the fast-paced, globally interconnected world of today.

CHAPTER 2

ESTABLISHING A FIRM FINANCIAL BASIS

Long-term stability, mental tranquility, and the capacity to accomplish life's objectives all depend on having a strong financial base. Without it, financial stress can take over your life, making it hard to concentrate on developing yourself or to take advantage of possibilities. The main components of creating a solid financial foundation—budgeting, saving, and investing will be discussed in this chapter. These components are the cornerstones of future wealth and financial stability.

2.1 Successful Budgeting

The first step to financial discipline is making and following a budget. By enabling you to match your spending to your objectives and make sure you are not living over your means, budgeting gives you financial control.

The following are some tips for making a sustainable budget that supports your objectives:

A well-crafted budget is a road map for reaching your financial goals, not just a list of spending. Determine your monthly income and fixed costs (loans, rent, and utilities) first. After that, set aside money for essentials like groceries and transportation, then indulge in leisure activities like going out to eat or entertainment. A useful guideline is the 50/30/20 rule:

- You should set aside 50% of your income for needs, 30% for discretionary expenditure, and 20% for debt repayment and savings.

This approach guarantees that your budget stays sensible, balanced, and represents your priorities.

The significance of monitoring your spending and making necessary adjustments:

Making a plan is only the first step in budgeting; ongoing monitoring and modification are also necessary. Spreadsheets and smartphone apps are two tools that might help you keep track of all your expenses. Reviewing your spending on a regular basis enables you to see trends, pinpoint wasteful behaviors, and make the required corrections. For instance, you can choose to cook more frequently at home or make fewer non-essential purchases if eating out is taking up too much of your cash. Maintaining financial discipline is a lifelong endeavor, and your budget should adapt to your changing needs.

Methods for handling debt and steering clear of financial hazards:

An essential component of budgeting is debt management. Credit card bills and other high-interest obligations can easily get out of control, consuming your income and leaving little left over for investments or savings. Start with smaller debts for faster gains (the snowball method) or prioritize paying off high-interest loans first (the avalanche method). Limit your credit card use and stay within your budget to prevent taking on new debt. By setting up an emergency fund (covered below), you may prepare for unforeseen costs and steer clear of financial hazards like taking on new debt when life throws you a curveball.

By avoiding typical financial pitfalls, a well-structured budget enables you to take charge of your financial destiny and come closer to your objectives.

2.2 The Secret to Long-Term Stability: Savings

The foundation of financial stability is savings. They allow you to plan for future objectives without taking on needless risks and act as a cushion for unforeseen costs. One of the most important steps in creating a strong financial foundation is developing sound saving practices.

The importance of saving and the process of creating an emergency fund:

One of your main financial priorities should always be saving because it offers a safety net in an emergency. The purpose of an emergency fund is to cover unanticipated costs, including unexpected medical bills, auto repairs, or a sudden loss of employment. Three to six months' worth of living expenses should be saved in a conveniently accessible account, according to financial experts. In an emergency, this fund makes sure you don't have to rely on loans or credit cards, which could lead to long-term debt.

If you have to start small, start consistently. Even a modest monthly savings contribution from your paycheck can add up over time and establish a buffer of funds that will give you peace of mind and protection from life's unforeseen events.

Different savings account types and strategies for optimizing returns:

Savings accounts are not all made equal. Based on your objectives, it's critical to select the appropriate account type:

1. **Basic savings account**: Usually has lower interest rates but provides simple access to your money. This works well for short-term savings or your emergency fund.
2. **High-yield savings account:** These accounts are a superior choice for longer-term savings because they offer higher interest rates than traditional savings accounts.
3. **Deposit Certificates (CDs):** Though your money is locked in for a set amount of time (usually six months to five years), certificates of deposit (CDs) offer better interest rates than savings accounts. If you don't need to access your money right away, this

is a fantastic alternative.

4. **Money market accounts:** These accounts balance accessibility and earnings by offering higher returns than standard savings accounts and the ability to write checks.

Selecting the appropriate account guarantees that your funds are there when you need them and helps you optimize the returns on your savings.

Savings and short- and long-term financial objectives should be balanced:

While emergency savings are vital, it's also critical to save for long-term goals (like retirement) and short-term ones (like a new car or vacation). Create distinct savings accounts, or "buckets," for various objectives in order to accomplish this successfully. Establish monthly recurring payments to these accounts to automate your savings. In this manner, you're continuously achieving all of your financial objectives without having to give it any thought.

Making sure that your short-term and long-term savings are balanced can help you be ready for the years to come as well as the near future.

2.3 Putting Money Into Your Future

The next step is to start investing when you've established a strong savings base. While investing enables your money to increase over time, assisting you in achieving long-term prosperity and financial freedom, saving is essential for preserving liquidity and getting ready for immediate demands.

The fundamentals of investing and how to begin accumulating wealth:

The goal of investing is to make your money work for you by producing returns that are higher than inflation and aid in the gradual accumulation of wealth. Determine your risk tolerance first, taking into account your time horizon and financial objectives. For example, you can afford to take on more risk by investing in equities if you're saving for retirement thirty years from now. You might want to think about safer options like bonds or mutual funds if your goal is closer, like purchasing a home in five years. The secret to risk management is diversification, which involves distributing your investments over several asset types (stocks, bonds, and real estate).

If required, begin modestly by establishing a brokerage account, looking into robo-advisors, or making contributions to an IRA or 401(k) retirement plan. The power of compound interest will work in your favor the earlier you begin.

Examining various investment vehicles, such as mutual funds, equities, bonds, and real estate:
In a well-rounded portfolio, every investment instrument has a distinct function:
1. Although they are more volatile, stocks offer the best chance for long-term gain and represent ownership in a company.
2. Bonds, which are essentially loans to governments or businesses, are a more steady choice for conservative investors since they pay interest on a regular basis and are less risky than equities.
3. Real estate is a good option for anyone seeking physical assets with the potential for sizable long-term profits because it offers both income (via

rent) and prospective appreciation.

4. Mutual funds and exchange-traded funds (ETFs) are groups of stocks or bonds that are pooled together; they provide diversification and a lower level of risk than investing in individual equities. ETFs track indexes passively and frequently have cheaper costs than mutual funds, which are actively managed.

You may create a diversified portfolio that fits your financial objectives and risk tolerance by knowing the part that each asset class plays.

The way compound interest benefits you over time:
One of the most effective strategies for accumulating wealth is compound interest. It describes the interest you receive on both the principal the original investment and the interest that accrues over time. Your money increases in value over time as you earn interest on your interest. Because of its exponential growth, even modest initial investments might eventually yield substantial returns.

Because of the power of compounding, an investment of $1,000 with an annual return of 8% may increase to nearly

$10,000 in 30 years. Time is of the essence; the earlier you begin, the more you stand to gain from this "snowball effect."

The first step to long-term stability and wealth building is laying a strong financial foundation. You position yourself for financial success by becoming an expert at budgeting, saving money, and making smart investments. Your financial security today and readiness for the future are guaranteed by a methodical approach to money management that is based on a budget, bolstered by savings, and enhanced by investment.

CHAPTER 3

FINANCIAL DEVELOPMENT AND CAREER ADVANCEMENT

Your long-term performance and financial development are greatly influenced by your career. You may greatly improve your financial independence by choosing your work path wisely, aggressively seeking opportunities for development, and looking into side gigs or entrepreneurship as additional sources of income. This chapter will explore how to strategically advance your career to guarantee both financial success and professional fulfillment.

3.1 Selecting a Professional Route for Monetary Achievement

One of the most important choices you will make for your financial future is choosing the correct career. A carefully considered job choice can offer long-term growth prospects, financial stability, and personal fulfillment. The secret is to match your professional goals with your hobbies and market demands, and to make a commitment to lifelong learning.

Determining industries with high demand and professions with room to grow:

Not every industry offers the same growth potential or financial rewards in the quickly changing employment market of today. Researching sectors that are expected to expand and pay competitively is crucial. Industries with a lot of room for growth and high salaries include technology, healthcare, renewable energy, and financial services. For instance, because of our growing reliance on technology, jobs in data science, cybersecurity, and software engineering are highly sought after and pay well.

Think about things like employment stability, anticipated industry development, and career advancement opportunities while deciding on a career path. By focusing on expanding industries, you put yourself in a position to take advantage of future demand.

The function of education, skill enhancement, and

lifelong learning:

Many times, your educational background and the abilities you bring to the table determine how much money you make in your job. Although many well-paying occupations require a college degree, it's also critical to think about the return on investment (ROI) of your degree. Gaining a degree or certification in an area with significant room for expansion might lead to increased pay and employment prospects.

But learning doesn't end after you graduate. Maintaining your relevance in your line of work and increasing your earning potential require constant learning. Invest in yourself by learning new technology, keeping abreast of industry developments, and obtaining certifications that increase your marketability. Professional workshops, certificates, and online courses can all help you develop new abilities and increase your marketability.

How to match profitable professional prospects with personal passions:

It's commonly believed that if you pursue your passions, you won't have to work a day in your life. However, financial success is not always guaranteed by enthusiasm alone. Finding the point where market demand and your own interests converge is crucial. A career in software development or artificial intelligence, for example, might provide both financial success and personal fulfillment if you have a strong interest in technology.

Determine professions that give significant financial advantages and let you capitalize on your passions and talents. This connection guarantees that you create a secure financial future in addition to enjoying your career.

3.2 Ascending the Corporate Ladder

After deciding on a career path, long-term financial growth depends on performing well in your current role and moving up the organizational ladder. Higher pay, greater benefits, and more work security are all associated with career development.

Methods for achieving success at work and getting promoted:
It's crucial to continuously deliver excellent work and show

your worth to the company if you want to advance up the corporate ladder. This is going above and beyond the call of duty to take on extra duties that demonstrate your initiative and leadership abilities. Within your organization, establish a reputation for dependability, creativity, and problem-solving.

Additionally, look for mentorship opportunities to acquire knowledge from seasoned experts who can offer direction and assistance. Take the initiative to ask for and utilize feedback from your managers and coworkers in order to enhance your performance. You raise your chances of getting promoted by showcasing your dedication to both professional and personal development.

The following are some tips for building a solid professional network that will help you advance your career:

- One of the main factors influencing career success is creating a strong professional network. Networking gives you access to important information, opens doors to new chances, and puts you in touch with prominent people in your field. To expand your network, participate in professional associations, go to industry events, and use websites like LinkedIn.

- You can get employment leads, information about industry trends, and career guidance from mentors, sponsors, and colleagues in the field. Be in the company of individuals who push you to develop professionally and who provide you chances to do so. Building meaningful relationships that assist your long-term professional development is the goal of networking, not just getting to know individuals.

Salary and benefit negotiations to optimize financial growth:

When it comes to pay and perks, many professionals undervalue the importance of negotiating. Nonetheless, throughout the course of your career, negotiation can greatly raise your earning potential. Examine industry norms to determine what a reasonable offer is for your position and experience level before engaging in wage negotiations. You can obtain this information with the aid of websites such as Glassdoor, Payscale, and LinkedIn Salary.

Prioritize your value and contributions to the business when negotiating. Be ready to share concrete instances of how your efforts have benefited the company. In order to enhance your remuneration package, you could also think about bargaining for extra advantages like bonuses, stock options, chances for professional growth, and flexible work schedules.

You can position yourself for higher financial success throughout your career by developing the crucial skill of negotiation.

3.3 Entrepreneurism and Side Projects

Investigating side projects or starting your own business can help you advance your profession, create extra revenue streams, and accelerate your path to financial freedom. In addition to increasing wealth, income diversification provides stability during unpredictable times.

Investigating side projects to supplement your full-time work:

With the stability of full-time work, side gigs are a common way to augment income. You can use your current abilities or explore new interests outside of your main employment with a lot of side projects. For instance, freelancing as a consultant could be a profitable side gig if you work in marketing. If you're a gifted writer, you might want to create a blog or do freelance writing.

Effective time management and making sure your side business doesn't conflict with your primary work are essential for its success. Select a side project that fits your interests and skill set and that you can work on at your own pace. Finding clients and showcasing your skills is made simple by websites like Upwork, Fiverr, or Etsy.

Converting loves and pastimes into lucrative ventures:
For people who want to make their interests their full-time employment, entrepreneurship is an alluring alternative. A lot of prosperous business people began by turning a pastime into a company. There are innumerable methods to make money from your hobbies and talents, whether they are fitness coaching, graphic design, photography, or baking.

To determine your unique selling proposition (USP) and comprehend your target market, do extensive market research prior to launching your company. A carefully considered company plan is necessary for success. Prioritize developing a strong brand, offering your clients value, and gradually growing your business.

Although starting a business involves risk and work, there can be significant financial and personal rewards. It enables you to take charge of your earnings, follow your interests, and leave a lasting legacy.

The following are some ways that entrepreneurship might expedite financial independence:
One of the most effective paths to financial freedom is entrepreneurship, which has the potential for limitless financial growth. Operating your own business gives you the freedom to choose your own earning potential, unlike standard positions with fixed salary. Higher incomes, more flexibility, and more time management are common benefits of being a successful business.

Additionally, entrepreneurship offers the chance to develop assets that can produce steady income, such products, intellectual property, or a clientele. Additionally, having a business allows you to generate a variety of revenue sources, such as royalties or passive income from investments.

But there are hazards associated with entrepreneurship, so proper planning is crucial. Risk management, financial knowledge, and flexibility are all essential components of successful entrepreneurship.

Financial growth and career advancement are tightly related. You can quicken your journey to financial independence by picking a vocation that fits with your financial objectives, performing well at work, and investigating side projects or business endeavors. You can attain both professional success and financial independence by taking a proactive approach to work progression, learning new things constantly, and looking into other sources of money.

CHAPTER 4

Managing Financial Risks

Managing financial risk is essential to accumulating and preserving wealth. Even while financial progress frequently receives more attention, safeguarding your assets and income against unanticipated difficulties is just as crucial. This chapter will examine how insurance, prudent decision-making, and emergency preparedness can be used to strategically reduce financial risks. You can preserve long-term stability and protect your financial future by being aware of and controlling these risks.

4.1 The Significance of Insurance in Budgeting

In order to safeguard your wealth and offer stability in the face of life's unforeseen events, insurance is essential. The correct insurance plans can shield you and your family from financial disaster in the case of an accident, health crisis, or property damage.

Comprehending the many forms of insurance (life, health, property, etc.):

There are various kinds of insurance, each intended to safeguard a distinct area of your financial life. Among the most prevalent kinds are:

- In the event of illness or accident, health insurance can drastically lower out-of-pocket spending by covering medical charges. Considering how expensive healthcare is in many nations, it's one of the most important kinds of protection.
- In the case of your passing, life insurance offers your dependents financial help. It guarantees that in the event of your untimely death, your loved ones won't have to deal with debt or unstable finances.
- Your home and personal possessions are protected by property insurance against loss or damage from natural catastrophes like floods, fires, or theft. This protection is advantageous for both tenants and homeowners.
- Disability insurance replaces your income in the event that a sickness or disability prevents you from working.

Costs associated with auto accidents, damage, or theft are covered by auto insurance.

Every kind of insurance covers particular risks and contributes to your overall financial plan. You can cover different aspects of your life by combining these plans according to your own needs.

How insurance protects your financial future from unanticipated circumstances:

Providing a safety net in times of disaster is one of insurance's primary goals. An unexpected medical emergency, for example, can lead to enormous medical expenses. This might wipe away your money or possibly put you in debt if you don't have health insurance. In a similar vein, if you are unable to support your family financially, a life insurance policy guarantees that they will be able to pay for living expenses, debts, or schooling.

You can transfer risk to an insurance business by using insurance as a tool. In return for the assurance that you won't be left to bear the financial load alone in the worst case scenario, you pay premiums. Long-term financial planning needs this protection because it makes sure that unforeseen circumstances won't sabotage your efforts to accumulate wealth.

The cost-benefit comparison between underinsurance and sufficient coverage:

It's critical to weigh the amount of coverage you require against the cost of insurance premiums. While having too much insurance could mean you're paying for unnecessary coverage, having too little insurance can expose you to serious financial concerns. To carry out a cost-benefit evaluation:

- **Evaluate your financial responsibilities:** Take into account your assets, potential liabilities, and dependents to ascertain what you need to safeguard.
- **Assess the likelihood of danger:** For instance, property insurance cannot be negotiated if you reside in a region that frequently experiences natural disasters. However, you might not require comprehensive life insurance if you are childless.
- **Compare coverage options and costs:** Different insurance companies charge different prices for different levels of coverage. Find the best deal by comparing policies and shopping around.

Making sure your insurance coverage is sufficient and reasonably priced will provide you peace of mind without breaking the bank.

4.2 Avoiding Financial Pitfalls

Common financial errors have the potential to destroy even the best-laid financial plans. You can safeguard your wealth and preserve your financial stability by being aware of these dangers and taking proactive measures to stay clear of them.

Typical financial errors and how to prevent them:
The following are some of the most common financial blunders:
1. **Living beyond your means:** One guaranteed way to get into debt and unstable finances is to spend more than you make. Living within your means and creating a realistic budget are crucial.
2. **Ignoring the need to save:** Many people don't prioritize saving, which might make them exposed in times of need or financial crisis. Whether it's for

retirement, major expenditures, or unforeseen costs, saving should always come first.

3. **The failure to make retirement plans:** Financial instability later in life can result from failing to make contributions to a retirement plan early in your employment. Even in modest sums, it is imperative to begin retirement savings as soon as feasible.

It takes self-control, awareness, and proactive money management to avoid these errors.

The risks associated with high-interest debt, particularly credit card debt:

High-interest debt, especially from credit cards, is one of the largest financial traps. Interest rates on credit cards are frequently much higher than those on other kinds of loans, and accruing a balance month after month can quickly result in crippling debt.

1. **The accumulation of interest:** It can be challenging to pay off the principal if you're only paying the minimum payments because interest can mount up. Compound interest allows what began as a small balance to increase tremendously over time.

2. **The spiral of debt:** A vicious cycle of continuously paying interest on high-interest debt without making any headway on principal reduction can result. Your future borrowing options may be restricted as a result, and your credit score may suffer.

To prevent this, make it a priority to pay off high-interest debt as soon as you can and refrain from taking on more debt than you can safely handle. You can control your spending and stay out of the credit card trap by creating and following a budget.

Identifying financial warning signs and addressing them:

It's critical to identify early indicators of financial difficulties so that you can take action to address them before they worsen. Red flags to be aware of include:

1. **An increase in debt levels:** You should review your spending and debt repayment plans if you find that your debts are increasing rather than decreasing.
2. **Missed payments:** Missed or late payments on credit cards, loans, or bills may be a sign that you're spending more than you can afford.

3. **No savings for emergencies:** You run the danger of experiencing financial instability in the event of an emergency if you don't have at least three to six months' worth of living expenses saved.

Early intervention is essential for these problems. Regain control over your finances by prioritizing saving, reducing wasteful spending, and creating a debt repayment plan.

4.3 Emergency Financial Planning

Emergencies can occur even with insurance and cautious budgeting. Having a financial safety net is essential for navigating difficult times without sacrificing your long-term financial objectives, whether they are caused by unforeseen house repairs, a medical emergency, or a job loss.

Establishing a safety net for finances: the function of emergency funds

- An emergency fund is a savings account set aside especially for unforeseen costs. It acts as a safety net, enabling you to pay for crises without using up all of your long-term resources or taking on high-interest loans.

- The amount that can be saved: Generally speaking, financial advisors advise saving three to six months' worth of living expenditures. This guarantees that you can continue living your way of life in the event of an emergency, such as losing your job or incurring significant medical costs.
- Where should I store it? You should have easy access to your emergency fund in a money market or high-yield savings account. Your emergency fund will maintain its worth while still being accessible for quick use thanks to these alternatives' liquidity and low interest rates.

Even in the face of unforeseen difficulties, having an emergency fund in place provides you with financial stability and peace of mind.

How to foresee and get ready for unforeseen costs or financial downturns:
It's prudent to plan for possible financial downturns, such as recessions or industry-specific slowdowns, in addition to

emergency cash. Plan appropriately by taking into account how changes in your industry or worldwide economic trends may impact your revenue.

- **Cut back on discretionary spending:** Reducing non-essential purchases during uncertain times can help you save money and preserve resources.
- **Create new sources of income:** During economic downturns, diversifying your revenue streams through investments, side gigs, or passive income sources can offer additional stability.

Your overall financial health can be less affected by financial emergencies if you prepare for these scenarios in advance.

Diversifying sources of income to protect against economic uncertainty:

It might be dangerous to rely just on one source of income, particularly when the economy is unstable. Creating several revenue streams will help you diversify your income and lessen the impact of unforeseen expenses.

- Diversified income streams include the following examples: In order to supplement your main job, think about looking into side jobs, rental income, dividend-paying securities, or freelance work. Your financial security will be less reliant on any one source if you have a varied array of revenue sources.

You may lower your risk and improve your financial resilience by proactively creating a variety of revenue sources.

A crucial component of long-term financial planning is risk management. You can safeguard your money and build a safety net for your family by getting the right insurance, staying away from typical financial hazards, and being ready for any emergency. In addition to protecting your financial well-being, strategic financial risk management sets you up for long-term success and growth.

CHAPTER 5

DEVELOPING LIFELONG FINANCIAL MANAGEMENT SKILLS

Long-term financial success is based on prudent money management. Mastering money management in the complicated financial environment of today requires utilizing technology, forming sound financial practices, and, when required, getting professional advice. This chapter explores the key elements of effective financial management and shows you how to make smart, well-informed decisions to take charge of your financial future.

5.1 Tools and Software for Personal Finance

Personal financial management has never been easier or more effective in the digital era. You can keep on top of your financial goals more easily by streamlining your investing, saving, and budgeting processes with the aid of personal finance software and tools.

The best applications and tools for investing, saving, and creating a budget:

Numerous personal finance solutions are available to make certain facets of money management easier. The following are a few of the best tools and applications:

- **Budgeting apps:** Users may classify spending, make budgets, and track income and costs in real-time with the use of tools like Mint, YNAB (You Need A Budget), and PocketGuard. They assist you find areas where you may make savings by providing insights into your spending habits.
- **Saving apps:** Digit and Qapital make saving easy by automatically transferring small amounts into your savings account. They enable you to save money without having to worry about the cost of bigger transactions.
- **Apps for investing:** Robinhood, Acorns, and Betterment allow users to easily invest in equities, exchange-traded funds, or retirement funds. By streamlining the investment process and providing educational materials, these platforms serve both inexperienced and seasoned investors.

Your financial objectives and personal preferences will determine which tool is best for you. These tools can assist in automating and optimizing your financial plan, regardless of your focus on investing, saving, or budgeting.

How technology can help you manage your finances more efficiently:

People may now manage their money more effectively than ever thanks to technology, which has completely changed personal finance. Personal financial software reduces the possibility of human error and saves time by automating processes like bill payment, savings transfers, and investment contributions. Furthermore, a lot of apps provide real-time alerts, which let users know about spending limitations, transaction activity, and account balances.

- For instance, investing with a robo-advisor such as Betterment enables you to optimize for tax savings and balance your portfolio automatically without requiring active management. In a similar vein, a budgeting program such as YNAB may offer you comprehensive reports that give you a clear picture of your financial situation.

Among the main advantages of utilizing personal finance technology are automation, analytics, and real-time data accessibility. With the help of these capabilities, customers may make proactive financial decisions based on current, reliable data.

The significance of keeping an eye on financial trends and making decisions based on data:
Keeping up with the latest developments in personal finance and financial markets might mean the difference between financial success and failure. By keeping an eye on inflation rates, stock market trends, interest rates, and economic indicators, people can modify their financial plans as necessary. For instance:

1. Refinancing debt or buying a home can be beneficial when interest rates are low, but saving in high-yield accounts may seem more alluring when interest rates are high.
2. **Stock market trends:** Keeping an eye on market trends can assist investors in making well-informed choices regarding the timing of asset purchases and

sales.

Because it eliminates biases and emotional decision-making, data-driven decision-making is crucial to financial management. Better results can be obtained by using statistics to inform your decisions, whether you are thinking about making an investment or reviewing your savings plan.

5.2 Building Sound Financial Practices

The foundation of long-term financial security is sound money management practices. You can stay on pace to reach your financial objectives by adopting consistent, disciplined spending, investing, and saving habits.

The value of consistency in prudent spending, investing, and saving: One of the most effective personal financial strategies is consistency. Over time, little, consistent efforts can have a big impact. For instance:
1. **Saving:** Even if the sums are modest, setting up automated savings transfers guarantees that a percentage of your salary is consistently saved aside.

These little donations might add up to a sizable emergency fund or retirement savings over time.

2. **Investing:** You can benefit from dollar-cost averaging by consistently investing a set amount each month, regardless of market conditions. By distributing your assets over time, this technique reduces the impact of market swings.

3. **Spending wisely:** You can prevent needless debt and build money by using thrifty spending practices and regularly adhering to a budget. Making better financial decisions involves avoiding impulsive purchases and emphasizing value over price.

Instead of depending on intermittent efforts, the secret to long-term financial success is to do the correct things consistently over time.

How to replace unproductive financial habits with productive ones:

It takes awareness, discipline, and strategic planning to break negative financial habits. Impulsive spending, failing to save, and debt accumulation are examples of common negative behaviors. To stop these behaviors:

1. **Determine the triggers**: If impulsive buying is an issue, observe the circumstances or feelings that lead to these choices. Do you shop more when you're bored or under stress? You can steer clear of these trends by being aware of them.
2. **Establish new routines:** Adopt healthier habits in place of unhealthy ones. Establish a meal plan or designate a certain "fun" budget if you frequently overpay on eating out in order to keep costs under control.
3. **Use tools for accountability**: By monitoring your spending and warning you when you're approaching your spending caps, personal finance apps can assist you in maintaining accountability.

It takes time to break negative habits, but long-term financial development results from substituting them with constructive ones, such as regular saving and prudent spending.

Realistic financial goal-setting and progress monitoring:

One of the most important steps in money management is

setting specific, reachable financial goals. Setting clear objectives gives your financial decisions direction, whether you're saving for a down payment on a house, debt repayment, or retirement savings.

1. **SMART goals:** Financial objectives are to be Time-bound, Relevant, Specific, Measurable, and Achievable. For instance, a SMART goal may be, "I want to save $10,000 for a house down payment in two years by saving $420 per month," rather than, "I want to save money."

2. **Monitoring progress:** To track your progress toward your objectives, use spreadsheets, savings calculators, or budgeting programs. Reviewing your money on a regular basis keeps you motivated and enables you to make necessary adjustments.

Your financial path can be mapped out with goal-setting, and you can stay on course by monitoring your progress.

5.3 The Function of Financial Consultants

When it comes to guiding people through difficult financial decisions, financial advisors are crucial. Professional guidance can be very helpful when creating a thorough financial plan, managing investments, or preparing for retirement.

When and why to seek advice from a financial advisor:
There are some times in life when seeking financial advice can be especially helpful. These consist of:

1. **Retirement planning:** It is important to make sure you have a sustainable income plan and sufficient funds as you get closer to retirement. You may choose the best retirement funds, optimize your Social Security benefits, and project your future needs with the assistance of a financial counselor.
2. **Investment management:** An advisor can offer tailored investment strategies based on your objectives and risk tolerance if your portfolio becomes complicated or you are uncertain how to strike a balance between risk and profit.
3. **Big life events:** Getting married, purchasing a home, or inheriting money are all important financial turning points that could call for professional advice. Financial advisors assist you in making well-informed choices that complement your

long-term financial strategy.

When your financial situation becomes too complicated for you to handle alone or you want to be sure that you're making the greatest choices for your future, speaking with a financial advisor can be very helpful.

Comprehending the advantages of professional financial planning guidance:

Financial advisors provide a number of significant advantages, such as:

1. Advisors offer objective guidance that is based on your financial objectives and situation. When emotions or uncertainty influence your decision-making, this objectivity is helpful.
2. In order to develop a well-rounded strategy, advisors take a comprehensive approach to your financial situation, taking into account all facets of your life, such as income, taxes, debt, and investments.
3. **Long-term approach:** Advisors prioritize long-term, sustainable financial planning over short-term gains. They assist you in developing plans for accumulating, preserving, and allocating

wealth.

The knowledge of a financial advisor may give you clarity and confidence in your choices, whether you need assistance with investments, retirement planning, or tax strategies.

The following are some tips for selecting the best advisor for your unique financial circumstances:

A critical first step in optimizing the advantages of professional advice is choosing the appropriate financial advisor. When selecting a consultant:

1. A high degree of knowledge and commitment to professional standards are indicated by qualifications such as Chartered Financial Analysts (CFAs), Certified Financial Planners (CFPs), and others.
2. **Take a look at their pricing schedule:** Financial advisors can bill by the hour, a fixed fee, or a portion of the assets they manage. Make sure the advisor you select has a pricing schedule that fits your goals and financial constraints.
3. **Consider their experience:** Advisors are more likely to offer pertinent and useful advice if they

have worked with people in comparable financial circumstances to your own.

4. **Request references and testimonials:** You can get a feel of the advisor's track record and client satisfaction by reading reviews or talking to previous clients.

In addition to having expertise, the ideal advisor should be someone you can trust to look out for your best financial interests.

Developing sound financial management skills takes a lifetime and calls for the appropriate resources, routines, and direction. Using personal finance tools, creating sound financial practices, and getting professional help when needed can help you create a strong financial basis going forward. You will be prepared to ensure your financial well-being and accomplish your financial objectives if you have a well-defined plan in place.

CHAPTER 6

MANAGEMENT AND REMOVAL OF DEBT

Both a burden that restricts your economic potential and a tool for financial success are possible with debt. Achieving long-term objectives and preserving financial stability depend on efficient debt management. This chapter will cover the many forms of debt, effective ways to pay it off, and how to stay out of debt after you've paid it off. You can take charge of your money and lay the groundwork for a safe future by becoming an expert in debt management.

6.1 Comprehending Various Debt Types

Debt is not all the same. While some types of debt might help you accumulate wealth, others can get out of hand and cause long-term financial hardship. Being able to distinguish between good and bad debt and spotting possible debt traps is essential to prudent money management.

The distinction between bad debt (like credit cards) and good debt (like mortgages):

- **Good debt** is debt that benefits you by enabling you to purchase assets that appreciate in value over time or that enhance your financial status. For example, homeownership is made possible by mortgages, and the value of the property may increase. In a similar vein, student loans may be a wise investment if they help you develop the skills necessary for a higher-paying job.
- The term "bad debt" often refers to debt that is taken on for consumption, frequently with exorbitant interest rates and no chance of financial return. One of the best examples is credit card debt, particularly if it builds up from pointless purchases and is not paid off in full each month. Due to the high interest rates on credit card balances, people may find themselves in a situation where they end up paying far more than they initially borrowed.

Knowing the difference enables you to make well-informed borrowing decisions and guarantees that you only take on debt that benefits your long-term financial goals.

Strategic ways to use leverage to increase wealth: Leverage is the use of borrowed funds to raise the possible return on investment. Leverage may be a very effective instrument for accumulating money if applied properly. For instance:

1. **Investing in real estate:** By taking out a loan to buy a home, you can take advantage of tax deductions, rental income, and property appreciation while only having to pay a fraction of the total cost up front through a mortgage.
2. **Business financing:** Taking out business loans to invest in new projects, buy equipment, or grow operations might result in profits that outweigh the cost of borrowing.

Making sure that the possible returns from the borrowed funds exceed the costs of the loan, including interest payments, is crucial to using leverage efficiently. Careful preparation is necessary since poorly managed leverage might result in financial issues.

Identifying high-interest traps and predatory lending practices:

Predatory lenders take advantage of borrowers by providing loans with unjust or abusive terms. People who are financially vulnerable are frequently the targets of these tactics, which result in crippling debt. Among the warning indicators are:

1. Payday loans and certain high-interest personal loans can put debtors in debt cycles by charging outrageous interest rates that make it hard to pay off the balance.

2. **Hidden costs and penalties:** Some lenders employ intricate contracts that contain hidden fees, which makes it simple for borrowers to accumulate more debt.

3. The practice of a lender pressuring a borrower to refinance an existing loan repeatedly with no benefit to the borrower, which leads to greater fees and longer debt, is known as "loan flipping."

Reviewing loan conditions carefully, being aware of your rights as a borrower, and consulting with reliable financial consultants prior to signing any loan agreements are all necessary to prevent predatory lending tactics.

6.2 Debt Repayment Techniques

A methodical approach that enables you to make progress without feeling overburdened is necessary for debt repayment. The avalanche and snowball approaches are two of the most often used debt repayment strategies, and each has special benefits. Additionally, by lowering interest rates and streamlining payments, debt consolidation and refinance might offer relief.

The avalanche vs. snowball approaches to debt repayment:

The snowball strategy focuses on making minimum payments on higher bills while paying off your lowest debts first. You start with the smallest loan and work your way up to the next one, which creates a "snowball" effect as each obligation is paid off. When you witness rapid development, this strategy increases motivation and momentum.

In contrast, the avalanche method reduces the total amount

of interest paid over time by giving priority to paying off the obligations with the highest interest rates first. This approach is the most economical way to lower debt, but it could take longer to see noticeable results.

Your financial circumstances and personal tastes will determine which of these two approaches you choose. It might be better to use the snowball method if you're driven by immediate gains. The avalanche strategy, however, provides the biggest financial advantage if lowering interest payments is your top concern.

How to effectively prioritize and handle multiple debts:
It can be daunting to manage several debts, but you can recover control by using a methodical approach. Here's how:
- Depending on whether you're utilizing the avalanche or snowball strategy, you can either list all of your obligations by interest rate or from least to greatest.
- To ensure that you continue to make the minimum payments on all of your obligations and concentrate additional funds on your priority debt, create a budget that allots a portion of your income to debt

repayment.
- Reduce wasteful spending and use the money saved to settle your obligations more quickly.
- By monitoring your progress and acknowledging your accomplishments along the way, you can maintain your discipline.

Setting debt payback as a top priority according to a well-defined plan guarantees effective debt management without causing needless financial strain.

Consolidation and refinance options to lessen debt burdens:

Consolidation is the process of consolidating several loans into one loan with better terms or a lower interest rate. Replacing a current loan with a new one, frequently at a reduced interest rate, is known as refinancing. Both choices might lessen your total debt load and make debt repayment easier.

You can pay off multiple bills at once with a debt consolidation loan, which reduces your monthly payment to one. Over time, this might lower your interest payments and make management simpler.

Transferring high-interest credit card debt to a card with reduced rates is possible with balance transfer credit cards, which offer promotional periods with low or no interest. High-interest obligations, such as mortgages or student loans, might benefit greatly from refinancing. You can lessen the total amount paid over the course of the loan by negotiating a lower interest rate.

Weighing the advantages and disadvantages of these choices is crucial, though. After the promotional time expires, balance transfer cards frequently return to higher interest rates, and some consolidation loans have fees or lengthier payback terms. Make sure that any consolidation or refinance fits with your long-term financial objectives.

6.3 Preventing Recurrence of Debt

The next task after successfully paying off your debts is to prevent getting into debt again. You may maintain a debt-free lifestyle and create long-term financial stability by comprehending the root reasons of excessive spending and forming sound financial practices.

The following are some tips for living within your means and preventing debt recurrence:

Self-control and meticulous budgeting are necessary. Setting aside funds for investments and savings while keeping spending in line with income is crucial. To do this:

1. **Make a reasonable budget** that covers both discretionary spending and all essential costs, including housing, food, and transportation.
2. To make sure you're remaining inside your budget, regularly track your spending.
3. To avoid having to use credit cards or loans to pay unforeseen costs, it is advisable to establish an emergency fund.

You can lower your risk of taking on additional debt by intentionally spending less than you make and avoiding lifestyle inflation.

The psychology of excessive spending and strategies to avoid it:

Psychological factors including emotional triggers, peer pressure, or the need for rapid pleasure are frequently the causes of excessive spending. Knowing the psychological factors that contribute to excessive spending can assist you in creating countermeasures:

1. **Spending on emotions:** A lot of people use shopping as a coping mechanism for boredom, stress, or anxiety. Find healthy coping strategies, like working out, practicing meditation, or interacting with others, to prevent this.

2. **Inflation in lifestyle and peer pressure**: It's simple to feel under pressure to maintain a greater level of life than peers or coworkers. To resist, put more emphasis on your own financial objectives than on comparisons with others.

3. **Impulsive purchasing:** Establish a "cooling-off period" before making non-essential purchases to prevent impulsive purchases. This allows you to consider whether the purchase is essential or in line with your financial objectives.

You can maintain financial management and prevent debt by being more self-aware of these psychological aspects.

Establishing routines that promote long-term financial well-being:

Developing sound financial practices is crucial to keeping a debt-free lifestyle. Among the crucial behaviors are:

1. **Automating investments and savings:** Configure automatic deposits into your retirement and savings accounts. This makes it easier to accumulate wealth over time by ensuring that saving comes before consumption.

2. **Reviewing your money on a regular basis:** Arrange for regular financial check-ins to go over your budget, evaluate your progress toward your objectives, and make any required corrections.

3. **Educating yourself on personal finance:** You may make better financial decisions and steer clear of problems by consistently learning about investing, money management, and financial planning.

By establishing these habits, you may lower your risk of relapsing into debt and confidently pursue your financial objectives, laying the groundwork for long-term financial stability.

Achieving financial freedom requires effective debt management and repayment. You may take charge of your financial destiny by comprehending the many forms of debt, creating efficient repayment plans, and forming routines that stop debt from happening again. Regardless of whether you're trying to pay off debt or

Long-term financial success requires a disciplined approach to debt management in order to prevent taking on new debt.

CHAPTER 7

Long-Term Financial Planning

The foundation of stability and financial security is long-term financial planning. It includes planning for important life events, safeguarding retirement, and using estate planning to ensure your family's well-being in addition to handling daily expenses. This chapter explores the key elements of long-term financial planning, such as tax optimization, estate planning, and retirement preparation. You may create a financial roadmap that guarantees stability and wealth preservation for many years to come with careful planning and foresight.

7.1 Retirement Planning

Many people look forward to retirement, but early and thorough planning is necessary for financial security in this stage of life. You may create a solid retirement plan that supports a happy, financially secure future by being aware of your alternatives and making wise selections early on.

The importance of early retirement preparation for financial stability

One of the most crucial elements of effective retirement planning is getting started early. Your savings will have more time to increase through compound interest if you start saving early. To achieve the same retirement goal, for instance, a person who begins saving in their 20s will need to make fewer monthly contributions than a person who begins in their 40s. Furthermore, early planning enables you to modify your savings plans over time in response to shifting income, market conditions, and changing financial objectives.

The following are some of the main advantages of early retirement planning:

1. **Compounding growth:** Over time, the compound interest impact can cause even modest contributions to increase dramatically.
2. **Adaptability to change:** As your financial circumstances change, you can alter your retirement schedule, investment plans, or savings rate.

3. **Decreased stress:** The fear of running out of money as retirement draws near is lessened with early planning.

Comprehending the various retirement account options (401(k), IRA, etc.): Retirement savings vehicles such as 401(k)s and IRAs provide long-term growth prospects and tax benefits. Your retirement savings can be maximized by selecting the appropriate account type for your circumstances. Among the most popular choices are:

- Employer-sponsored retirement plans, such as 401(k)s, enable you to make pre-tax contributions that lower your current taxable income while increasing tax-deferred until withdrawal. Matching contributions, or free money for retirement, are provided by many employers.
- A traditional individual retirement account (IRA) is one in which contributions may be tax deductible and taxes are postponed until retirement, when the money is taken out.
- **Roth IRA:** It is a desirable choice for people who anticipate being in a higher tax band later in life because contributions are paid with after-tax income

and withdrawals are tax-free in retirement.
- **The Simple and Sep IRAs:** These accounts, which have larger contribution limits than standard IRAs, are intended for independent contractors or small business owners.

Because each form of retirement account has unique tax advantages, contribution caps, and withdrawal guidelines, it's critical to select the ones that best suit your financial circumstances and retirement objectives.

How to figure out how much you'll need to have a decent retirement:

Your current income, anticipated retirement lifestyle, health care requirements, and longevity all affect how much you need for retirement. A retirement fund should, as a general rule, be able to replace **70-80% of your pre-retirement income** per year. Financial counselors and retirement calculators are two ways to accomplish this.

Important factors to take into account are:
1. **Expenses, both present and future:** Calculate how much housing, utilities, health care, travel, and

leisure will cost you each month once you retire.

2. When estimating the future cost of living, take inflation into consideration. Over time, prices will rise, and your savings must also stay up.

3. Planning for a retirement that lasts 20–30 years or longer is crucial due to the increased life expectancy.

When it comes time to retire, you can make sure you're on pace to fulfill your financial needs by establishing a clear retirement savings goal and periodically reviewing it.

7.2 Estee Planning and Will Creation

Not only the wealthy should prepare their estates. To guarantee that their assets are allocated in accordance with their desires and to shield their loved ones from legal issues, everyone regardless of income level should establish an estate plan. Effective estate planning guarantees that you keep control of your assets even after you pass away and lessens the tax burden on heirs.

The significance of safeguarding your possessions and preparing your estate:

Organizing your financial affairs to ensure that your assets are safeguarded and allocated in accordance with your desires is known as estate planning. State rules will determine how your assets are distributed if you don't have an estate plan, which might not be what you want. Your loved ones will be taken care of, your taxes will be reduced, and any legal issues will be avoided with estate planning.

An estate plan's primary elements are as follows:

1. **A will:** A legal document that outlines the distribution of your assets and names the executor of your estate.
2. **Trusts:** A legal structure that gives you more control over the timing and distribution of assets and enables you to transfer assets to beneficiaries in a tax-efficient way.

In the event that you become disabled, choose someone to handle your financial or medical affairs using a power of attorney.

The process of drafting a will and selecting beneficiaries:

The cornerstone of an estate plan is a will. It designates guardians for minor children if necessary and guarantees that your assets are allocated in accordance with your intentions. Take into account the following when creating a will:

- List all of your assets, including real estate, investments, bank accounts, and personal possessions.
- Determine who will inherit your assets and how they will be distributed by selecting beneficiaries. To prevent misunderstandings or disagreements, be explicit and precise in your instructions.
- **Appoint an executor:** Choose a reliable individual to administer the distribution of your estate, settle debts, and carry out the terms of your will.

Review and amend your will on a regular basis, particularly following big life events like marriage, the birth of a child, or a change in your financial circumstances.

Implications of inheritance for taxes and ways to reduce them:

Inheritance may result in tax liabilities, such as income taxes on specific asset classes and federal and state estate taxes. By reducing these taxes, careful estate planning can increase the amount of money that is transferred to your heirs.

1. **Estate taxes:** Estates over a specific amount are subject to the federal estate tax, which is now over $12 million for individuals. However, smaller estates may be impacted by state-imposed estate or inheritance taxes.
2. **Capital gains taxes:** When inherited assets, such as stocks or real estate, are sold, they may be liable to capital gains taxes; however, the tax burden may be lessened because the basis is often increased to the original owner's death value.
3. **Trusts:** By creating a trust, you can provide beneficiaries access to your assets while reducing inheritance taxes and having more control over how they are allocated.

Professionals in estate planning can assist you in structuring your estate to ensure that your assets are dispersed as planned while lowering the tax burden on your heirs.

7.3 Optimization and Tax Planning

A crucial component of long-term financial planning is tax planning. You may put strategies in place to reduce your tax burden and optimize wealth growth by being aware of how taxes affect your income, assets, and retirement. Utilizing tax-advantaged accounts, investment plans, and deductions to lower your tax liability and create a stable financial future are all part of effective tax planning.

Recognizing how taxes affect your wealth and income:
Almost every element of your finances is impacted by taxes, including your investments and income. Federal, state, and occasionally local taxes are usually applied to income in the United States. Furthermore, dividends, interest income, and capital gains from investments are all subject to various taxation. Optimizing your financial strategy begins with knowing your tax obligations.

Among the important tax factors are:
1. **Ordinary income tax:** This holds true for revenue

from self-employment as well as wages and salaries. Higher earners pay a higher proportion of their income in taxes because they are placed in higher tax brackets.

2. **The tax on capital gains:** This refers to the earnings from the sale of assets such as stocks or real estate. When assets are kept for more than a year, long-term capital gains are usually taxed at a lower rate than short-term gains.

3. **Interest and dividend income:** Depending on the source of income, investment income from stocks and bonds may be taxed at reduced eligible dividend rates or regular income rates.

You may organize your financial activities to reduce taxes and keep more of your profits if you know how each source of income is taxed.

Methods for lowering your tax liability with wise investments:

There are a number of ways to lawfully lower your tax liability while increasing your wealth:

1. **Investing in accounts that offer tax advantages:**

To lower taxable income now and increase long-term savings, use accounts such as Health Savings Accounts (HSAs), 401(k)s, and Individual Retirement Accounts (IRAs). Traditional retirement plan contributions reduce your taxable income, and the growth of your investments is tax-deferred until you take them out.

2. **Tax-loss harvesting:** This tactic lowers your taxable capital gains by selling investments that have lost value in order to offset profits from other investments.
3. **The municipal bonds are:** Municipal bonds are a desirable choice for higher-income investors wishing to lower their tax obligations because interest on them is normally excluded from federal income taxes and may also be deductible from state and local taxes.

You can drastically lower your tax liability by investing in tax-efficient ventures and selling assets at the right time.

Leveraging tax-advantaged accounts for retirement and savings:

Tax-advantaged accounts lower your tax liability while enabling you to save for retirement or other financial objectives. Among the most popular choices are:

1. **The Traditional IRA and 401(k):** Pre-tax contributions reduce your taxable income in the year they are made. When you withdraw money in retirement, ideally when you may be in a lower tax bracket, taxes are paid.

2. **Roth IRA:** It is a great choice for younger savers who anticipate being in higher tax bands later in life because contributions are paid using after-tax money and withdrawals are tax-free in retirement.

3. **HSAs (Health Savings Accounts):** The HSA offers a triple tax advantage (tax-deductible contributions, tax-free growth, and tax-free withdrawals for qualified costs). If you are eligible, you can contribute pre-tax money for medical expenses, and the money can be invested and grow tax-free.

Your long-term savings and investing plan can be greatly improved by making the most of tax-advantaged accounts, which can increase your retirement financial stability.

long-term financial planning is a thorough approach that incorporates tax optimization, estate planning, and retirement preparation. By comprehending and putting these ideas into practice, you may make a financial strategy that will safeguard your loved ones, secure your future, and optimize your economic potential. Keep in mind that every choice you make today creates the foundation for a safe and profitable tomorrow as you traverse your financial path.

CHAPTER 8

Juggling Finances and Relationships

It can be difficult to manage how relationships and money cross, but doing so is essential to preserving peace and respect between couples. The significance of financial independence in relationships, effective communication techniques, and conflict resolution techniques related to money are all covered in this chapter. Couples can create a solid basis for a happy, financially stable relationship by being aware of and taking care of these problems.

8.1 The Discussion of Money in Partnerships

Even though it might be awkward, talking about money with a spouse is essential to any relationship's success. Building confidence, avoiding misunderstandings, and guiding both spouses toward common financial objectives can all be achieved by being forthright and honest about money.

The following are some tips for having candid conversations with a partner concerning money:

It's important to approach starting a financial conversation with tact and compassion. To encourage fruitful dialogue:

1. **Select the appropriate time and location:** Steer clear of talking about money when you're feeling anxious or upset. Choose a serene setting where both partners are at ease.

2. **Engage in active listening:** Make sure that each spouse has a chance to voice their opinions and feelings regarding money. It shows respect and openness to listen without interruption.

3. **Employ "I" statements:** Instead of saying, "You always spend too much," frame conversations in terms of individual sentiments and viewpoints. For example, "I feel anxious about our spending habits." This method promotes comprehension and reduces defensiveness.

4. **Establish a routine for financial check-ins:** Having regular financial conversations can help mainstream and de-stigmatize the topic.

5. Establishing common financial goals and aligning

spending patterns as a pair can improve communication and foster a sense of cooperation. To match financial goals:

6. Establish both short-term and long-term objectives. Talk about your financial objectives, such as retirement planning, home ownership, or vacation savings.
7. **Together, create a budget:** By working together to create a budget, partners can better manage discretionary spending by understanding and agreeing on spending objectives.
8. **Hold each other accountable**: Evaluate your financial goals on a regular basis. To keep yourself motivated and committed, acknowledge and celebrate your accomplishments, no matter how tiny.

Identifying relationship financial red flags:
Recognizing possible warning indicators can assist in resolving problems before they become more serious. Here are a few warning signs related to finances:

1. **Secretive spending or saving behavior:** If one spouse keeps purchases a secret or avoids talking about money, it could be a sign of more serious

problems in the partnership.
2. Significant discrepancies in spending patterns can cause conflict, particularly if one couple believes the other is not managing their finances responsibly.
3. **Insufficient financial transparency:** Relationship mistrust and anxiety may arise if one partner refuses to divulge financial details.

Couples can address underlying problems and promote a better financial dynamic by identifying these warning signs early.

8.2 Keeping a Relationship Financially Independent

Maintaining a certain amount of financial independence is just as crucial in committed relationships as sharing money. It helps people maintain their identities, fosters security, and averts possible financial disputes.

The significance of maintaining a certain level of financial independence, even in committed partnerships:

Having financial independence enables people to preserve

their sense of autonomy and self-worth. It also acts as a safety net in the event of unanticipated events like divorce or separation. Important advantages include:

1. **Empowerment:** Possessing personal finances empowers people to make choices according to their values and objectives.
2. **Decreased conflict:** Keeping distinct assets or accounts can help reduce disagreements about priorities and expenditures.
3. The flexibility to handle personal costs without continually consulting a spouse is made possible by individual accounts.

How to strike a balance between personal financial objectives and joint expenses:

It takes preparation and open communication to strike a balance between personal and pooled finances. Think about the following tactics:

1. Establish how expenses will be distributed (e.g., equally or proportionally based on income) and decide which costs (e.g., rent, utilities, groceries) will be split by both parties by creating a joint budget.

2. **Assign personal spending allowances:** Every partner should have a certain amount for spending that they can do on their own without the other's consent.

3. **Regularly review the common goals:** Arrange for talks to evaluate shared financial objectives and make sure both spouses are at ease with their roles and contributions.

Establishing limits to avoid being financially dependent:

Financial boundaries must be set in order to prevent reliance, which can result in resentment and power disparities. Think about these methods:

1. The expectations for financial contributions should be discussed. Specifically, each partner's personal contributions to savings objectives and their share of expenses should be made clear.

2. **Keep separate accounts in addition to joint accounts:** This arrangement permits joint spending while maintaining individual financial autonomy.

3. Support one another's endeavors that improve personal financial independence and fulfillment,

such as hobbies, education, or professional advancement.

A partnership that cherishes both unity and uniqueness can be fostered by couples who work toward financial independence.

8.3 Resolving Conflicts, Love, and Money

Relationship tension frequently arises from financial disagreements. It's critical to comprehend efficient conflict resolution techniques in order to preserve peace and confidence.

Typical financial disputes in partnerships and strategies for resolving them:

Disparities in spending patterns, setting priorities for financial objectives, and debt management are a few typical financial disputes. To address these problems:

1. **Identify the root cause of conflicts:** Talk about the underlying problems that lead to financial disputes, like conflicting values or financial stressors.
2. **Make use of problem-solving strategies:** Instead of

assigning blame, approach disagreements as a team and come up with solutions together. Make an effort to reach agreements that honor the needs and viewpoints of both parties.

3. **Take into account expert advice:** If disagreements continue, consulting a couples therapist or financial advisor can help establish healthy communication techniques and offer an unbiased perspective.

The importance of trust and openness in shared finances:

Establishing trust in a relationship, particularly when it comes to money, requires transparency. Among the tactics to promote transparency are:

1. Frequent financial conversations: Maintain open lines of communication by talking about money updates, objectives, and difficulties on a frequent basis.
2. **Share financial documents:** Vital financial data, including credit reports, debt commitments, and income statements, should be accessible to both parties.

Build a relationship of mutual trust: Building trust takes

time. The connection will be strengthened overall if personal financial management is done with accountability and responsibility.

The following are some tips for drafting a reasonable financial agreement that pleases both parties:

A financial agreement specifies how partners will handle their money and settle any disputes that may arise. To establish a just agreement:

1. **Talk and work out terms:** Talking about their financial priorities and how to handle joint spending should involve both couples.
2. When drafting the agreement, take into account each partner's unique financial circumstances by taking into account their income, debt levels, and financial objectives.
3. **Regularly review and revise:** The financial arrangement should adapt to changing living conditions. Plan frequent check-ins to make sure it stays equitable and relevant.

Couples can successfully negotiate the challenges of money management and preserve their amicable relationship by encouraging open communication, honesty, and respect for one another.

Maintaining a healthy balance between relationships and finances calls for work, communication, and a readiness to work together to overcome obstacles. Couples can create a strong financial foundation that supports their common objectives and deepens their relationship by having honest conversations about money, staying financially independent, and resolving disagreements amicably. Partners can have a peaceful financial partnership that improves their personal and interpersonal well-being by working together and understanding one another.

CHAPTER 9

THE ECONOMIC EFFECTS OF IMPORTANT LIFE CHOICES

Your financial situation can be greatly impacted by important life decisions. Knowing the financial ramifications of your decisions is essential, whether you're thinking about purchasing a home, beginning a family, or going through life transitions like marriage or divorce. The costs of raising a family, the financial implications of purchasing versus renting, and how to modify your financial plans during major life transitions are all covered in this chapter.

9.1 Purchasing vs. Renting a Home

One of the most important financial decisions a person or couple may make is whether to rent or buy a property. Every choice has advantages and disadvantages that need to be carefully considered in order to choose the one that best suits your long-term objectives and financial circumstances.

The financial benefits and drawbacks of owning a property as opposed to renting:

The advantages of owning a home:
1. **Equity Building:** Over time, you may accumulate a sizable amount of equity in the home as each mortgage payment raises your ownership stake.
2. **Stability:** Unlike renting, where landlords have the power to raise rents, owning a home offers stability and predictability in housing costs.
3. **Tax Benefits:** Homeowners may be eligible for property tax and mortgage interest tax deductions, which lowers their overall tax liability.
4. **Personalization:** Being a homeowner enables upgrades and personalization, which can raise the value of a property.

The following are some drawbacks of homeownership:
1. **Upfront Costs:** Buying a property entails large upfront expenditures, such as down payments, closing costs, and moving costs.

2. **upkeep Responsibilities:** All repairs and upkeep are the homeowner's responsibility, which may result in unforeseen costs.
3. **Market Risk:** The value of real estate can change, and homeowners might find themselves in debt if the market drops.

Advantages of Renting:
1. One advantage of renting is that it allows you greater flexibility in terms of moving without the long-term commitment of a mortgage.
2. **Lower Upfront Costs:** Usually, renters just have to pay the security deposit and the first and last month's rent.
3. **No Maintenance Responsibilities:** Landlords take care of repairs and maintenance, saving tenants from unforeseen expenses.

Disadvantages of Renting:
1. **No Equity:** Rent payments add to the landlord's equity, giving the renter no return on their investment over the long run.
2. Periodically, renters may have to pay higher rent,

which might put a strain on their finances.
3. **Limited Control:** Renters frequently have limitations on how they can alter and personalize their living area.

How to evaluate your financial preparedness for homeownership: Prior to making the decision to purchase a home, evaluate your financial status using the following procedures:
1. **Check your credit score**: Getting a decent credit score is essential to getting a good mortgage rate. Get your credit report and, if needed, try to improve it.
2. **Find your DTI (debt-to-income ratio):** A DTI of 36% or less is usually preferred by lenders. Divide your monthly debt payments by your gross monthly income to determine your DTI.
3. Put money aside for a down payment. In order to avoid private mortgage insurance (PMI), aim for at least 20% of the home's buying price. To meet your down payment target, make a specific savings plan.
4. **Think about extra expenses:** Include recurring expenses like maintenance costs, homeowner's

insurance, and property taxes. To determine how affordable you are, make a budget that accounts for these costs.

Opportunities for long-term wealth accumulation through real estate investment:

Real estate can be a potent instrument for wealth accumulation:

1. In the past, real estate values have increased with time, giving homeowners a return on their investment.
2. **Rental Income:** Having rental properties can help you make passive income, which can help you grow your money overall.
3. **Tax Benefits:** Investing in real estate may offer tax advantages like capital gains exclusions upon sale and depreciation deductions.

When done strategically, real estate investing can result in substantial wealth gain, but it also takes considerable thought.

9.2 Financial Aspects of Beginning a Family

Although having a family is a happy and life-changing event, there are substantial financial obligations involved. Careful preparation and budgeting are necessary to be ready for these expenses.

The expenses of childrearing and financial planning:
Raising children can come with a significant financial burden in a number of areas:

1. **Direct Costs:** These comprise costs for things like clothing, food, childcare, and diapers. The U.S. The Department of Agriculture estimates that, excluding college costs, the cost of raising a child from birth to age 17 can surpass $233,000.
2. **Costs of Healthcare:** New parents must set up money for routine checkups, immunizations, and unanticipated medical costs. Take into account signing up for health insurance policies that provide coverage for pediatric care.
3. **Expenses of Education:** Start budgeting for future educational costs, such as college, K–12 education, and preschool. Look into 529 plans and education

savings accounts (ESAs), which provide tax benefits for education savings.

Budgeting for family holidays, medical care, and education:

Making a family budget entails setting aside money for a range of costs:

1. **Establish a Family Budget:** Monitor monthly earnings and outlays to pinpoint areas where expenses can be controlled. Add sections for leisure, education, healthcare, and childcare.
2. **Emergency Fund**: Create a sizable emergency fund to cover unforeseen costs associated with child rearing, guaranteeing financial stability in times of need.
3. **Organize Family Holidays:** To improve family bonding experiences, save aside money for family vacations. Think about giving priority to reasonably priced vacation options that enable significant experiences without going over budget.

How to strike a balance between future investments and savings and household expenses:

It's critical to strike a balance between short-term family demands and long-term financial objectives:

1. **Make Savings a Priority:** To guarantee that financial objectives are fulfilled, automate contributions to investment and savings accounts. This could contain general savings, education funds, and retirement accounts.

2. **Assess Lifestyle Decisions:** Take into account modifying your lifestyle to free up more money for investments and savings. This could be finding more economical ways to spend money on family activities or reducing non-essential spending.

3. **Together, talk about your financial objectives:** Make sure you and your partner are in agreement on future investments and family spending by having regular conversations about financial priorities.

Parents can give their kids a stable financial future by carefully budgeting for household spending and keeping an eye on long-term financial objectives.

9.3 Financial Planning and Major Life Transitions

Financial ramifications can be significant during life transitions like marriage, divorce, moving, or changing careers. To keep your finances stable and safeguard your possessions, you must be ready for these developments.

Financial consequences of preparing for marriage, divorce, or relocation:

Every one of these life events necessitates careful financial consideration:

1. **Marriage:** Talk to your spouse about your financial objectives and expectations. Think about setting up a shared financial vision, combining finances, and making joint budgets. Prior to marriage, candid conversations regarding finance and credit ratings are also essential.
2. **Divorce:** Recognize the financial effects of divorce, such as possible effects on credit scores, spousal support, and asset distribution. Seek guidance from a financial advisor or divorce lawyer to successfully manage the process.
3. **Relocation:** Take into account the financial effects of moving, including possible career possibilities, housing prices, and changes in the cost of living.

Before choosing, look into the housing and employment trends in the area.

How to preserve your financial assets during major life transitions:

Proactive planning is necessary to secure your financial assets:

1. Make sure you have sufficient insurance coverage to guard against unanticipated circumstances during life transitions by reviewing your insurance policies.
2. **Update Beneficiaries:** To reflect your current preferences, review and amend beneficiary designations on wills, retirement funds, and insurance policies.
3. **Seek Advice from Experts:** To handle complicated financial circumstances during transitions, consult with tax experts, attorneys, or financial advisors.

Flexibility in financial planning is essential for adjusting to new life circumstances.

Modifying financial plans to fit changing life circumstances:

1. **Regular Financial Reviews:** Arrange for frequent

check-ins to assess financial plans and make modifications in response to evolving objectives and needs.

2. **Create Contingency arrangements:** Make arrangements for unforeseen expenses that can occur due to life transitions like losing a job or experiencing health problems.
3. **Keep an emergency fund on hand:** Greater peace of mind throughout life changes can be achieved by having a healthy emergency fund, which can offer financial stability in unpredictable times.

You can handle big life transitions with assurance and stability if you are proactive and flexible in your financial planning.

Important life decisions need serious thought and preparation because they have a significant financial impact. People can make well-informed decisions that improve their financial well-being by being aware of the financial ramifications of purchasing a home as opposed to renting one, planning for the expenses of beginning a family, and modifying their financial plans during life transitions. You may create a secure financial future that supports your objectives and aspirations by being proactive with your preparation and communicating openly.

CHAPTER 10

THE PATH TO FINANCIAL INDEPENDENCE

Beyond just building wealth, achieving financial freedom is a life-changing experience. It includes knowing your financial objectives, being independent, and creating enduring habits that let you live a secure and confident life. The definition of financial freedom, the significance of becoming independent prior to major life commitments, and methods for maintaining long-term financial success are all covered in this chapter.

10.1 How to Define Financial Independence

In personal finance, financial freedom is frequently cited as the ultimate objective. Its definition, however, differs from person to person and entails a more thorough comprehension of your values, objectives, and lifestyle decisions.

What does it mean to be truly financially free, and how can one attain it? Financial freedom is the capacity to make decisions that are consistent with your values without being constrained by financial limitations. Usually, to reach this degree of freedom, one must:

1. **Debt elimination:** You can free yourself from the pressure of monthly payments by paying off high-interest debts like credit cards and personal loans.
2. **Creating a sustainable income:** Creating a variety of revenue streams, including investments, side projects, or passive income, offers flexibility and financial stability.
3. **Living below your means:** Developing a way of living that puts necessities before wants aids in conserving money and lessens financial strain.

The distinction between financial freedom and wealth:
Financial independence is the ability to make decisions for oneself, whereas wealth is frequently linked to substantial possessions and a high income. For instance:

- Financially free people may have enough assets and passive income to choose when and how to work, whereas wealthy people may be constrained by their investments or jobs, which can lead to stress and limit personal freedom.

- Regardless of income level, financial independence enables flexibility in life choices, including following passions, spending time with loved ones, and participating in community activities.

How to establish significant financial benchmarks for your journey:

Setting SMART (specific, measurable, realistic, relevant, and time-bound) goals is crucial to achieving financial freedom:

1. **Set short-term goals:** Concentrate on objectives that can be accomplished in a year, such as making a budget, paying off a certain debt, or saving a specified sum.
2. **Develop medium-term objectives:** Aim for achievements in the next two to five years, such as buying a house, launching a company, or saving money for emergencies.
3. **Establish long-term objectives:** Take into account objectives like retirement planning, leaving a legacy,

or reaching financial independence that will take place in five years or more.

Your financial path is mapped out by these milestones, which let you track your progress and make adjustments as needed.

10.2 Prior to falling in love, Achieving Financial Independence

Your personal and romantic lives can benefit from pursuing financial independence before getting into a committed relationship.

The beneficial effects of financial independence on interpersonal relationships:

Healthy relationships are promoted by financial independence since it:

1. **Reduces stress:** Relationships can be strained by financial concerns. Achieving independence frees people from outside influences and makes room for deeper relationships.
2. Being financially independent guarantees that both

spouses contribute to the partnership, which promotes respect and cooperation. This promotes equality.

3. Promoting candid communication: Talking about money becomes less emotional and more fruitful when both parties are financially stable.

The advantages of prioritizing your financial development before getting married:

1. Putting your financial development first might have several advantages.
2. **Clarity on personal values:** By concentrating on financial independence, you may make your values and the qualities you look for in a mate more clear, which will result in more compatible partnerships.
3. **Increased self-confidence:** Being financially independent boosts your self-worth and gives you the confidence to enter into relationships.
4. **Stronger relationship foundations**: Healthy dynamics and shared financial goals are made possible when you enter a partnership with no financial baggage.

How having financial stability allows you to confidently pursue love:

Having financial stability allows you to enter into partnerships without worrying about becoming financially dependent:

1. **Freedom to explore options:** When you are financially stable, you can freely explore possible partnerships without feeling compelled to do so, which promotes natural connections.
2. **Decision-making empowerment**: People who are financially secure are able to make choices that are consistent with their values and preferences instead of feeling pressured to make concessions for financial gain.
3. **Balance-setting**: Being financially independent gives you the ability to set limits in relationships, guaranteeing respect and understanding on the subject of money.

10.3 Maintaining Economic Achievement

Reaching financial independence is only the first step; maintaining it calls for hard work, ongoing education, and careful planning.

How to stay financially independent for the rest of your life:

Maintaining financial independence entails:
1. Regular financial reviews: Evaluate your financial status on a regular basis and modify your investment plans, savings objectives, and budgets to reflect evolving conditions.
2. **Adjusting to changes in life:** Financial planning must be modified in response to life events like marriage, having children, and changing jobs. Long-term success depends on taking the initiative to adapt to these changes.
3. **Creating an emergency fund:** Having a healthy emergency fund guarantees that you are ready for unforeseen costs without letting your financial objectives go by the wayside.

The significance of ongoing financial education and keeping abreast of trends:
Financial markets, regulations, and tactics are

ever-changing. Ongoing education is crucial:
1. To keep educated, take advantage of learning opportunities by reading financial literature, attending workshops, and subscribing to reliable financial news sources.
2. **Connect with financial professionals:** Making connections with peers, mentors, or financial advisors can help you gain knowledge and guidance that will improve your financial literacy.
3. **Remain flexible:** Be prepared to review and modify financial plans in reaction to fresh data, shifting market conditions, or individual situations.

Leaving a Legacy: How to Transfer riches and Financial Knowledge to the Next Generation:
1. Leaving a legacy entails not only transferring riches but also imparting financial knowledge.
2. **Teach your children about money management:** As your children become older, talk to them about budgeting, saving, and investing.
3. Establish a family financial plan by involving family members in financial conversations and encouraging an open and cooperative attitude around money.

4. **Create trusts or investment accounts:** To teach kids about investing and to safeguard their financial future, think about creating trusts or custodial accounts for them.

People can preserve their financial freedom and leave a lasting legacy that helps future generations by making these behaviors a priority.

Achieving financial independence is a complex process that calls for meticulous preparation, ongoing learning, and wise decision-making. You may confidently manage this journey by establishing your definition of financial freedom, putting it ahead of important life obligations, and putting mechanisms in place to maintain success. In the end, being financially independent allows you to follow your passions, live life as you see fit, and leave a lasting legacy for the people you care about.

ABOUT THE AUTHOR

 Renowned business strategist, author, and consultant James Royce Smartman has over twenty years of experience in a variety of fields, including corporate management, entrepreneurship, and finance. James has a strong academic background and an MBA from a prestigious university. As a result, he has a good understanding of the nuances of contemporary business practices and market dynamics.

James has held executive positions in multiple Fortune 500 businesses over his career, effectively leading projects that have sparked efficiency, growth, and innovation. Because of his special combination of theoretical knowledge and real-world experience, he can offer organizations of all sizes frameworks and concrete tactics.

James is regularly asked to speak at conferences and seminars as a thought leader in the business sector, offering his knowledge on subjects including strategic planning, organizational behavior, and leadership development. In addition, he frequently contributes his thoughts on new trends and best practices to eminent business journals.

James Royce Smartman is devoted to helping company executives and entrepreneurs realize their objectives by providing them with creative solutions and useful guidance. His writings seek to demystify difficult business ideas so that readers of all skill levels can understand and use them. James offers a road map for success that is in line with the changing business environment of today by emphasizing practical examples and tried-and-true tactics.

James regularly mentors young professionals and supports different business projects that foster entrepreneurship and innovation in addition to his writing and consulting work. He promotes an organizational culture that welcomes change and encourages expansion because he believes in the value of teamwork and ongoing education.

www.ingramcontent.com/pod-product-compliance
Lightning Source LLC
Chambersburg PA
CBHW050312230526
45471CB00005B/2143